The Planets

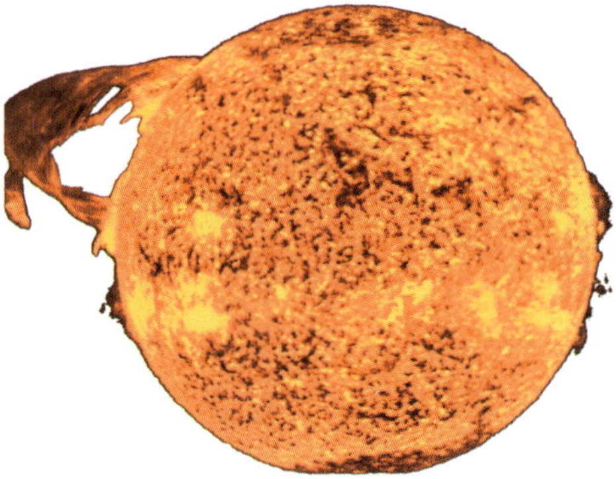

WELDON OWEN PTY LTD
Chairman: John Owen
Publisher: Sheena Coupe
Associate Publisher: Lynn Humphries
Managing Editor: Helen Bateman
Design Concept: Sue Rawkins
Senior Designer: Kylie Mulquin
Production Manager: Helen Creeke
Production Coordinator: Kylie Lawson

Text: Robert Coupe
Consultant: Dr John O'Byrne, Senior Lecturer,
Astronomy Department, University of Sydney

04 03 02 01
10 9 8 7 6 5 4 3 2

Published in New Zealand by Shortland Publications,
2B Cawley Street, Ellerslie, Auckland.
Published in the United Kingdom by Kingscourt Publishing Limited,
P.O. Box 1427, Freepost, London W6 9BR.
Published in Australia by Shortland–Mimosa,
8 Yarra Street, Hawthorn, Victoria 3122.

Printed in Singapore.
ISBN: 0-7699-0517-X

Contents

Early Astronomers

Since ancient times, people have studied the sky. They have used all kinds of instruments to work out the position of the stars and planets and to plot how they move. One early astronomer, a Greek named Ptolemy, said that the Earth stayed still and all the stars, including the Sun, moved around it. Then in 1543, almost 1,500 years later, a Polish astronomer named Copernicus suggested that the Earth and the other planets move around the Sun.

Early Telescopes

The first telescope, invented around 1590, was a simple spyglass. Less than 200 years later William Herschel built a huge telescope, like the one shown here.

Strange but True

Around 4,000 years ago, a circle of huge stone arches was built at Stonehenge in England. Scientists think people may have used these arches to show where the Sun and Moon would be on special days of the year.

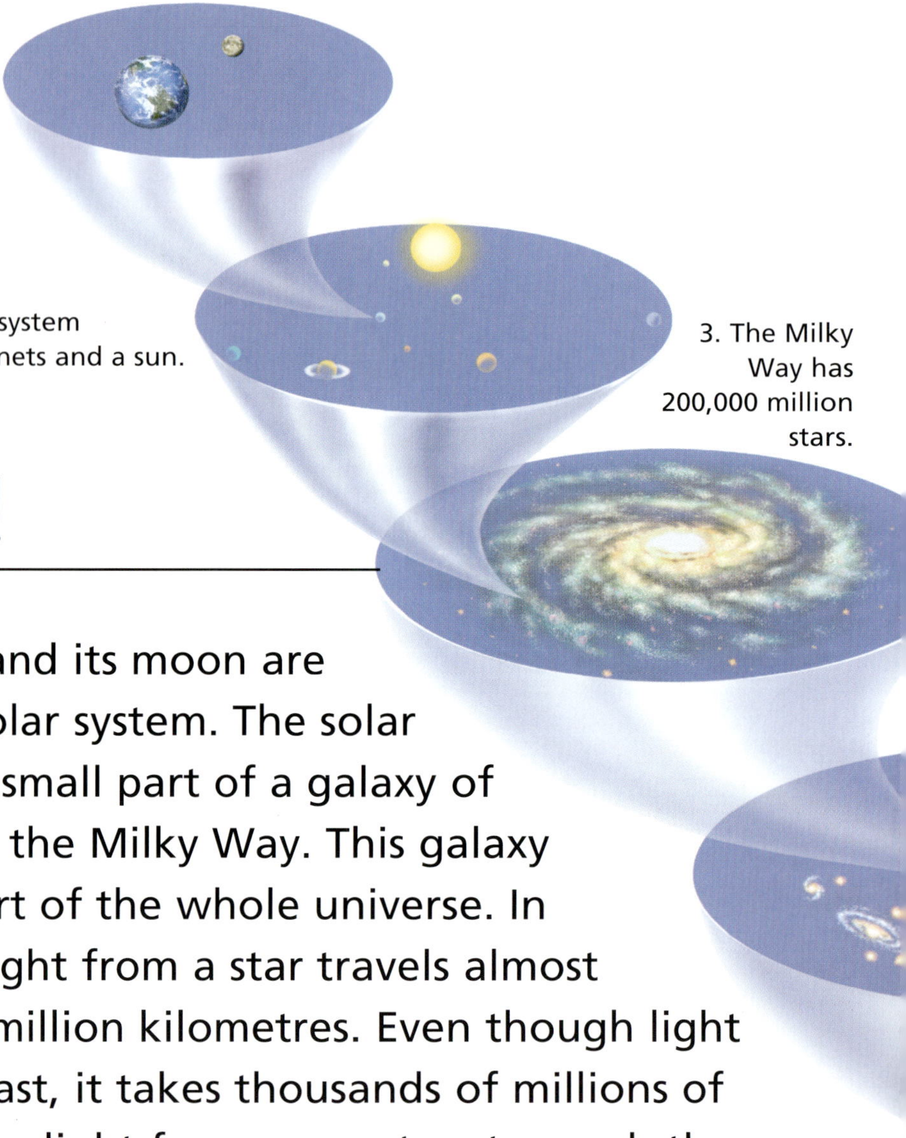

1. The Moon orbits the Earth.

2. Our solar system has nine planets and a sun.

3. The Milky Way has 200,000 million stars.

VAST!

The Earth and its moon are part of a solar system. The solar system is a small part of a galaxy of stars called the Milky Way. This galaxy is a tiny part of the whole universe. In one year, light from a star travels almost 10 million million kilometres. Even though light travels so fast, it takes thousands of millions of years for the light from some stars to reach the Earth. That's how vast the universe is!

Big Bang

Some scientists believe that the universe began millions of years ago with a big bang—and it's still expanding.

Make a Universe

1 Blow up a balloon to about the size of an orange.

2 Draw lots of small circles on the balloon. These represent galaxies.

3 Stand in front of a mirror and blow up the balloon. See your galaxies move further apart, just like real galaxies.

4. The Milky Way is one of a group of 30 galaxies.

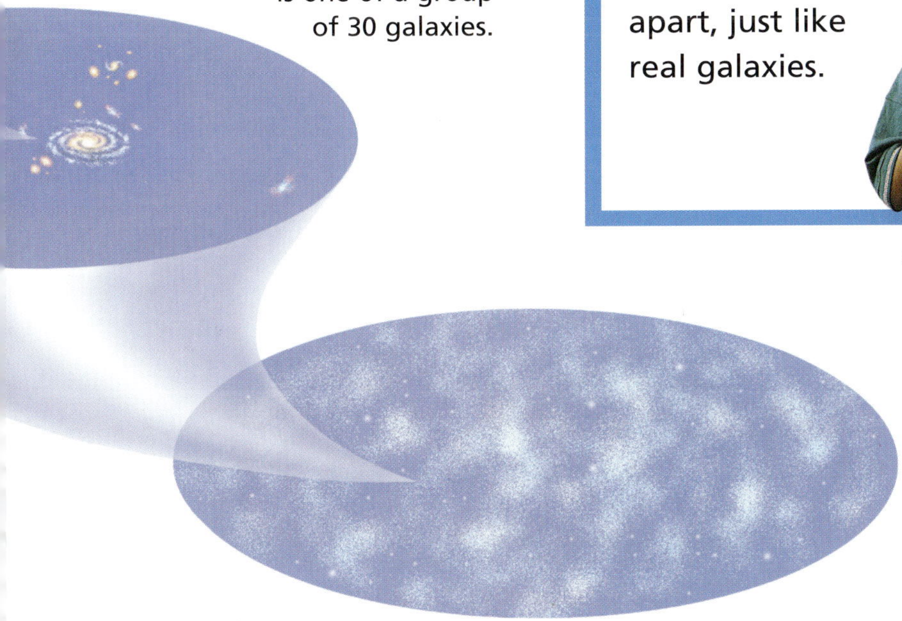

5. The Universe contains about 50,000 million galaxies.

Our Neighbours

A solar system has a star, or sun, at its centre, with planets orbiting around it. Our solar system has nine planets spinning around the Sun. Seven of these have one or more moons orbiting them. You can see most of the planets shining in the night sky. Large pieces of rock called asteroids and frozen balls of ice called comets also orbit the Sun.

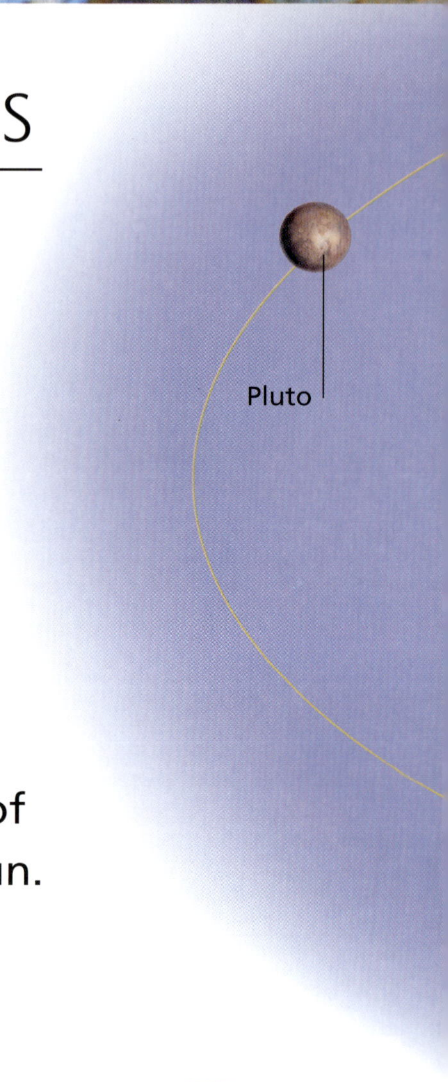

Gas and Dust
Our solar system was born when the Sun formed from a cloud of gas.

The Sun formed deep inside the dusty cloud.

A disc of gas and dust swirled around the infant Sun.

Bits of dust stuck together to form large pieces of rock.

The rocks bumped and stuck together to form huge rocky masses.

Over millions of years, these masses combined to form planets.

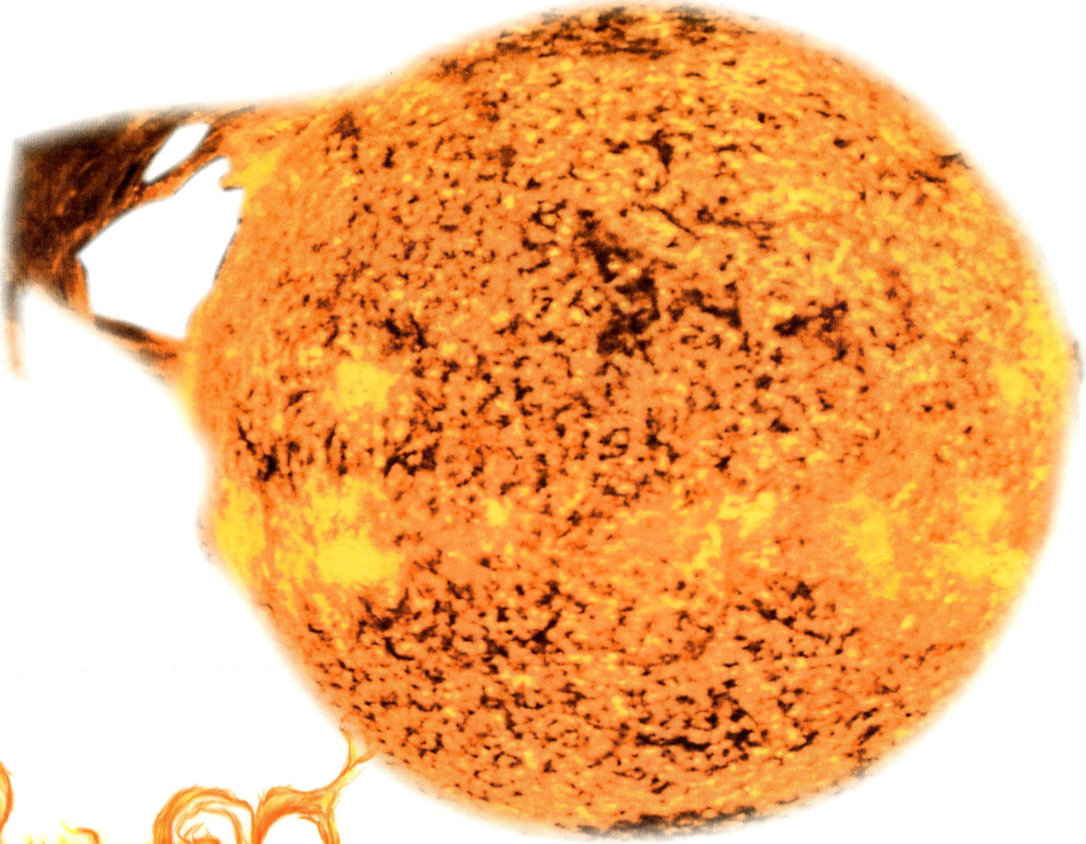

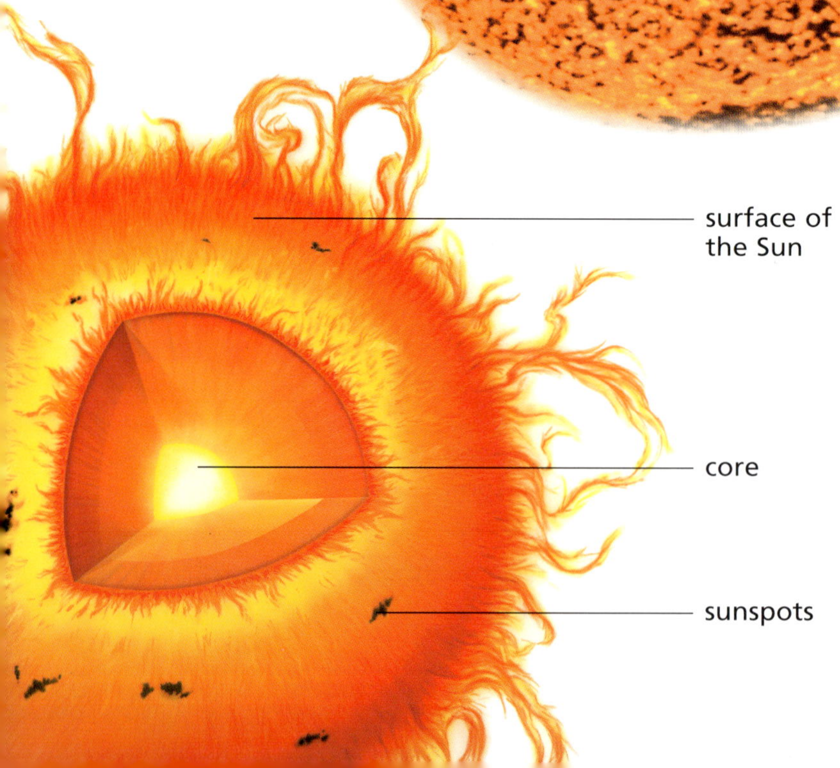

Solar Furnace

Heat and light spread out from the core—the hottest part of the Sun. Sunspots are cooler, darker areas on the surface of the Sun.

Our Sun

Astronomers believe that the Sun, the star at the centre of our solar system, is about halfway through its life. This huge ball of gases has existed for 5,000 million years, and it has enough hydrogen fuel in its core to last for that long again. When its fuel runs low, it will swell to a red giant and life on Earth will end.

Amazing!

Glowing bands of green light or arches of dancing light, called auroras, often appear at night in Arctic and Antarctic regions. They happen when particles from the Sun hit the Earth's outer atmosphere.

MERCURY AND VENUS

Mercury and Venus are hot planets, close to the Sun. Mercury can also be a very cold planet. It has no atmosphere to keep in its heat, and the temperature away from the Sun can be minus 200 degrees Celsius. Venus, at right, is the hottest of all planets and never cools down. It is surrounded by carbon dioxide, which traps the heat and keeps its surface boiling hot.

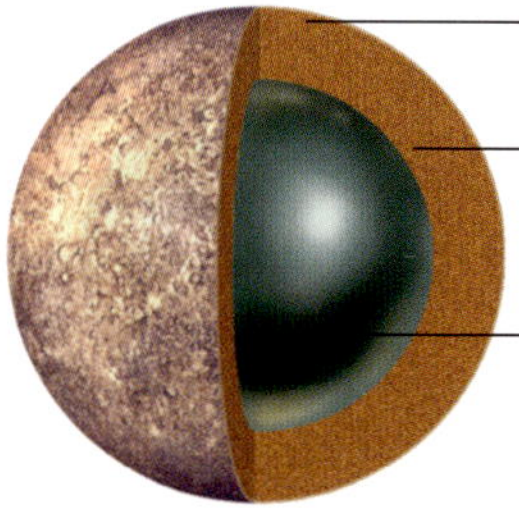

Rocky Mercury
Mercury's rocky surface is covered with deep craters. Beneath the rock is a core of iron and nickel.

Did You Know?

In Roman myths, Mercury was the messenger of the gods. In paintings he often has wings on his helmet and sandals to help him fly swiftly on his errands.

Earth History
Many scientists believe that life has developed on Earth over millions of years.

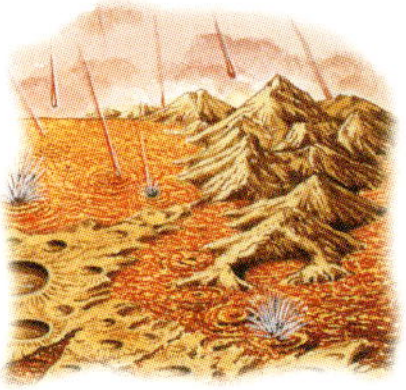

1. Too Hot
About 4,000 million years ago, the Earth was too hot for any life.

2. Early Ocean Life
About 3,800 million years ago, life began in the oceans.

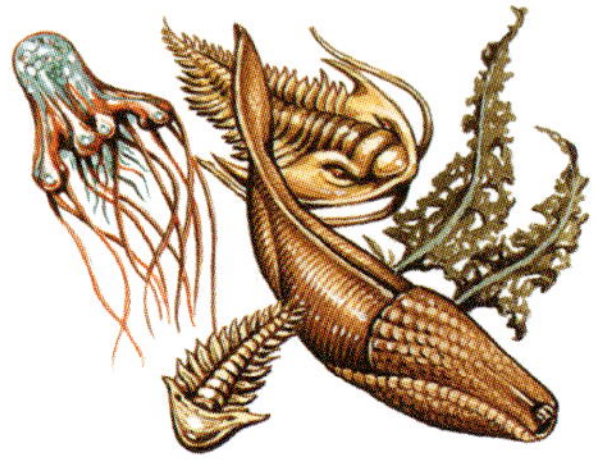

3. More Ocean Life
By 550 million years ago, the oceans were full of life.

4. The First Dinosaurs
Dinosaurs appeared 230 million years ago.

5. Early Humans
Humans date back to about 200,000 years.

The Earth

If you could look at the Earth from the Moon you'd see that most of the Earth's surface is covered with water. The Earth's plants and animals could not live without water. If the Earth were closer to the Sun, it would be too hot for water to exist. If it were further away, any water would be frozen as ice.

Our Moon

Look at the full Moon on a clear night and you will see dark patches. High mountains, deep valleys and wide craters filled with lava cast deep shadows on the Moon's sunlit surface. The uneven, rocky surface can be seen clearly in this picture, taken from one of the Apollo spacecraft that carried humans to the Moon between 1969 and 1972.

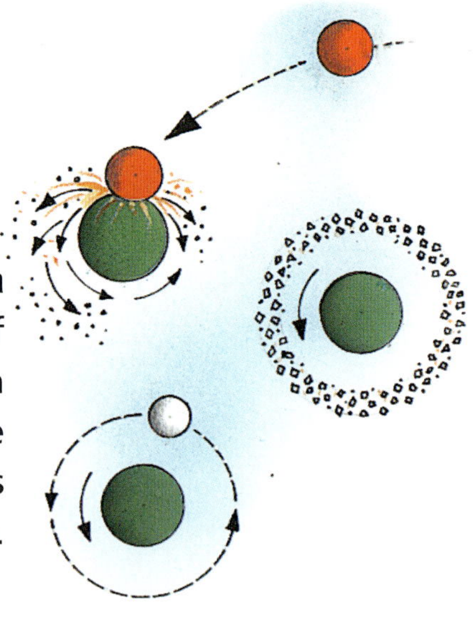

The Moon Is Born
Many scientists believe that millions of years ago the Earth collided with a smaller planet. Parts of the Earth's surface flew off into space. Eventually the pieces joined together to form the Moon.

Phases of the Moon

As the Moon orbits the Earth, we see different parts of its surface lit up by the Sun. Astronomers have given each of these phases its own name.

New Moon
The surface facing the Earth is in shadow—we can't see the Moon.

first quarter

waxing gibbous

Full Moon
The whole surface facing the Earth is lit.

waning gibbous

last quarter

waning crescent

AMAZING!

When astronauts circled the Moon in their spacecraft, they were able to watch the Earth rise and fall over the distant horizon just as we watch the Sun rise and set over the Earth.

Mars

A day on Mars is about as long as a day on Earth, and there are changing seasons. This has led people to ask whether anything could live there. Scientists now think that only the simplest forms of life could exist, since even the warmest days are extremely cold. Machines like the one at the right might help people study the surface of this dusty, red planet.

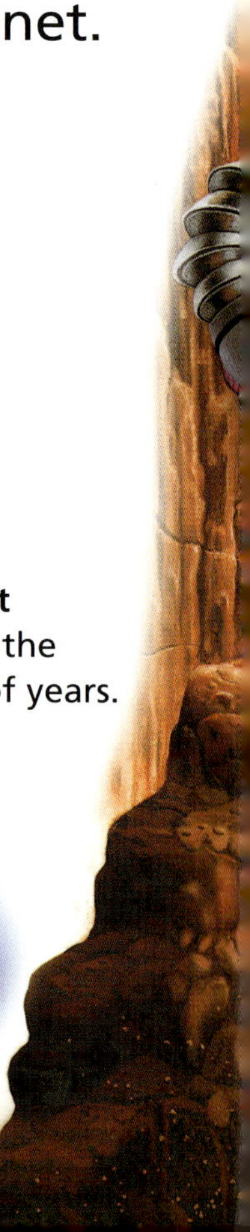

Arrivals from Mars

Pieces of rock that scientists believe are from Mars have been found on Earth.

1. The Take-off
An asteroid hits Mars. Pieces of rock fly out into space.

2. The Long Flight
These rocks orbit the Sun for millions of years.

3. The Landing
Some of the rocks hit the Earth's atmosphere and land as meteorites.

DID YOU KNOW?

There is a volcano on Mars called Olympus Mons which is as big as the American state of Arizona. Scientists think it's the largest volcano in the solar system.

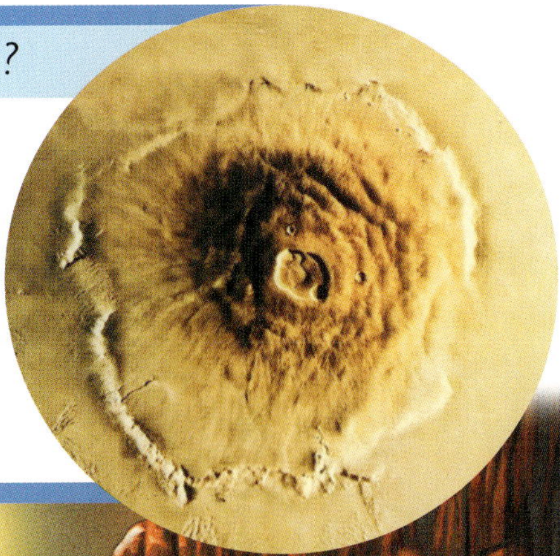

The Great Red Spot
Jupiter's surface consists entirely of gases. The Great Red Spot is a huge storm that never stops raging.

Many Moons
Four large moons and twelve small moons orbit Jupiter. The largest and brightest is called Ganymede.

JUPITER

Jupiter was the king of the ancient Roman gods, and the planet named after him is by far the largest in our solar system. It also spins the fastest—once every 10 hours—causing mighty winds and storms to rage around it. In 1994, fragments of a comet collided with Jupiter, causing flashes and dark scars that could be seen from Earth.

SATURN

Saturn is the second-largest planet in our solar system. Like Jupiter, it is a giant ball made of mainly hydrogen and helium. It spins almost as fast as Jupiter, and whips up winds many times as powerful as our fiercest cyclones. Thousands of coloured rings consisting of icy particles surround the planet. At least 18 moons move in orbit around Saturn.

Forming Rings
No one knows how Saturn got its rings. It's possible they formed after an asteroid crashed into one of Saturn's moons.

Collision
A comet or asteroid hits one of Saturn's moons.

Breaking Up
The moon shatters into icy clumps. These begin to orbit Saturn.

Closer View
From Earth, Saturn's rings look like three separate bands. In 1981 a space probe showed these three rings consisted of thousands of rings.

Spreading Out
The clumps break up into smaller particles, which spread out into a wide ring.

Rings and More Rings
Particles of different sizes form lots of separate rings.

Uranus

For many years, astronomers thought Saturn was the furthest planet from the Sun. Then, in 1781, the Englishman William Herschel discovered a new planet, twice as far from the Sun as Saturn. People realized that the solar system was much bigger than they had believed. Uranus, named after the Greek god of the sky, is a gas planet. It has narrow rings around it.

Miranda
Miranda, one of Uranus's moons, has deep ridges in its surface. It may once have broken apart, then joined together again.

Side-on Planet
Uranus is well known for being tilted on its side. An asteroid might have crashed into Uranus millions of years ago and pushed it over.

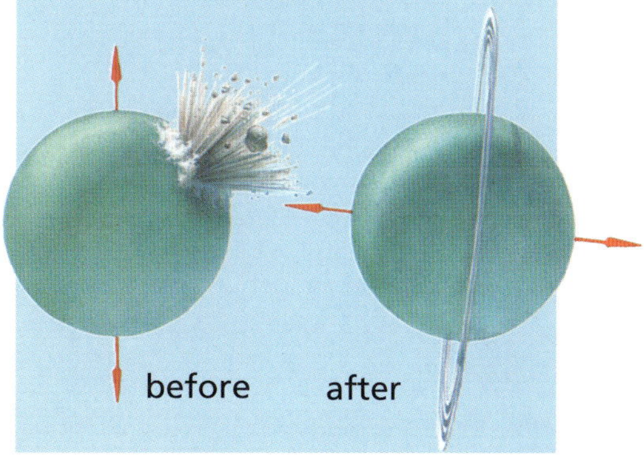

Neptune

Neptune is another gas planet surrounded by icy rings and it was only discovered in 1846. Here is Neptune as it would appear from Triton, the largest of its eight moons. The geysers on Triton's surface are fountains of frozen nitrogen gas. Neptune, named after the Roman god of the sea, looks blue because the methane gas that surrounds it soaks up red light and reflects blue light.

DID YOU KNOW?

There are only four places in the solar system that have active volcanoes—those that erupt. They are the Earth, Venus, Io (one of Jupiter's moons) and Triton. Liquid nitrogen erupts from the volcano craters on Triton.

Disappearing Great Dark Spot
In 1989, the space probe Voyager 2 photographed a huge storm in Neptune's clouds. Five years later, there was no longer any sign of it.

Dark Shadow

Charon and Pluto are close together. As it comes between Pluto and the Sun, Charon casts a deep shadow on Pluto's dim surface.

Pluto

Far away from the Sun in the outer parts of the solar system is Pluto. Pluto wasn't discovered until 1930. It is named after the Greek god of the underworld. Pluto is smaller than the Earth's moon, and is only about twice as big as its own moon, Charon. It takes Pluto almost 250 years to make its long orbit around the Sun.

Inside Pluto

Pluto and Charon are a mixture of rock and ice. Some of the outer ice turns to vapour when Pluto's orbit brings it close to the Sun.

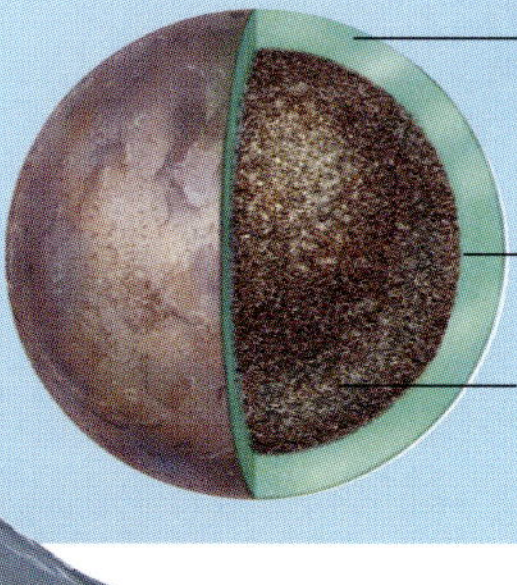

GLOSSARY

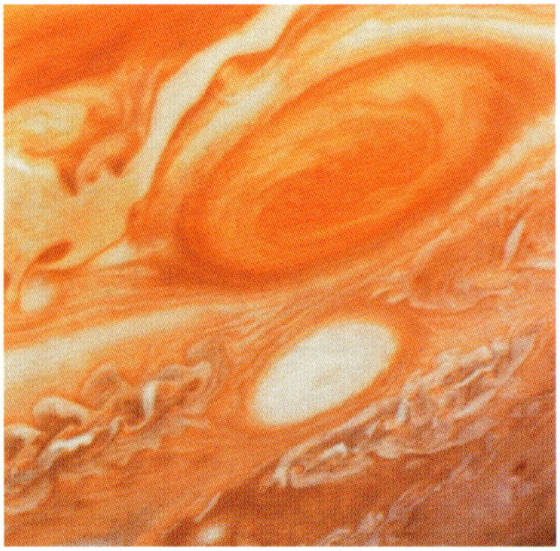

asteroid A large piece of rock or other material that moves in orbit around the Sun.

astronomer A scientist who observes and studies the stars, planets and the rest of the universe.

atmosphere The thin layer of gases that surrounds planets such as the Earth.

galaxy A huge collection of stars, planets, gas and dust. The Milky Way is one of many millions of galaxies in the universe.

gas planet A planet with a very deep atmosphere of swirling gases.

meteorite A piece of rock from space that travels through the Earth's atmosphere and that hits the Earth's surface.

moon A large body that moves in orbit around a planet. The Earth has one moon. Some other planets have many more.

planet A large body that moves in an orbit around a star. The Earth is a planet that moves around the Sun.

space probe A machine that is sent from the Earth to investigate and send back information about the surface and the atmosphere of other planets and moons.

Index

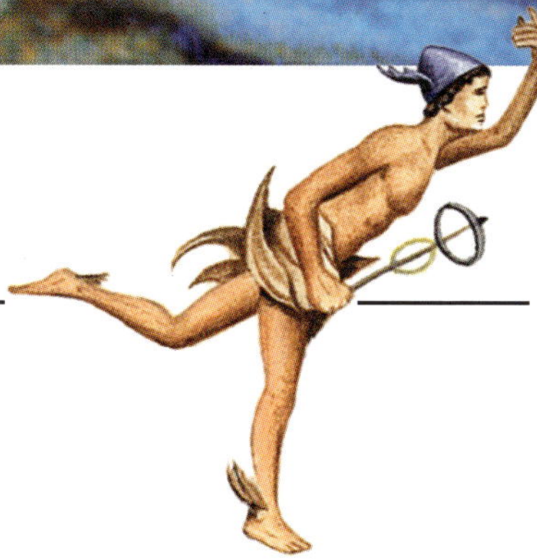

Credits and Notes

Picture and Illustration Credits
[t=top, b=bottom, l=left, r=right, c=centre, F=front, B=back, C=cover, bg=background]
Ad-Libitum/Michal Kanewski 7cr. **Corel Corporation** 5tr, 11br. **Digital Stock** 1c, 10tc, 16lc, 17c, 19tr, 20tl, 24–25bc, 27c, 30tc, 4–32 borders, FClc, Cbg. **Christer Eriksson** 12–13c, 18–19cr. **Murray Frederick** 14c, 14cr, 14tc, 14tr, 14cl. **Akira Fujii** 2l, 17r. **Lee Gibbons/Wildlife Art Ltd** 22bc, 22br, 23bl, 23br. **Ray Grinaway** 13tr, 31tr. **David A. Hardy/Wildlife Art Ltd** 3tr, 6–7c, 7tl, 8–9tc, 8–9bc, 12bl, 26–27bl, 29bc, FCtr. **Robert Hynes** 24c, 25br, BC. **Peter Mennim** 22–23c, FCc. **Darren Pattenden/illustration** 28tl, 28–29c. **PhotoEssentials** 20tr. **Oliver Rennert** 14–15rc. **Trevor Ruth** 21c, 27tr. **Ray Sim** 16br. **Marco Sparaciari** 4bc, 18cl, 18bc, 18br. **Steve Trevaskis** 4–5c. **Simon Williams/illustration** 10bl.

Acknowledgements
Weldon Owen would like to thank the following people for their assistance in the production of this book: Jocelyne Best, Peta Gorman, Tracey Jackson, Andrew Kelly, Sarah Mattern, Emily Wood.